CW00404504

TO SOME THEY'RE JUST SHEEP

Wendy Thompson
The Shepherdess In The Shed

From city to shepherdess.

Copyright @ 2023 Wendy Thompson

All rights reserved.

Cover Photo by Wendy Thompson

Other Photography by Wendy Thompson

No part of this book may be reproduced in any form or by written, electronic or mechanical, including photocopying, recording or by any information retrieval system without the written permission of the author.

Published by Wendy Thompson

Although every precaution has been taken in the preparation of this book, the author/publisher assume no responsibility for any omissions or errors. No liability is assumed for damages resulting from the use of information contained in this book.

ACKNOWLEDGMENTS

Firstly, thank you to my partner Jon, most definitely not a sheep farmer but who gave in to my persistence to have sheep, encouraged me to create my craft business and to finish this book. Without his patience and support, none of this would have happened.

I must include my dear friends, Gemma and Becca, who have listened to my tales of joy and woe and supported me throughout – the best friends anyone could have.

Further thanks to the farmer who gave me my first hands-on experience with sheep and to my friends, Jo who introduced me to Ouessants, Val who shares freely her wealth of experience, Guy for his skill and expertise, as well as Michelle, John and Chris for their continued support and encouragement.

This part would not be complete without acknowledging the work of our vets, especially Lucy who has always understood that to me they aren't just sheep and has done so much for us.

Of course, my final acknowledgment must go to my wonderful sheep, past and present, without whom my life would be very different.

FOREWORD

I am a shepherdess and fibre artist with my studio in a garden shed that overlooks my flock of sheep, hence "The Shepherdess In The Shed".

This book tells some of the story of how I left my life in the city and went on to become a vegetarian shepherdess with a small flock of sheep, all of whom will stay with me for the whole of their natural lives. There are tales of good times and bad times, with a bit of humour thrown in for good measure.

I am no literary genius but I hope you enjoy reading about us and the animals that make our life what it is.

CHAPTER 1

A POTTED HISTORY

If you had told me back in the eighties that I would end up a vegetarian shepherdess and fibre artist, I would have crossed a stocking clad leg, glanced at my expensive high heels, taken a sip of posh wine and laughed. I was in my twenties and having fun, or like a lot of us then, telling myself I was, when in reality we were fighting to keep our jobs in an unstable economic climate and with an uncertain future. Admittedly, I do still have a large collection of high heels and a few posh frocks, just in case, although, like me, they don't get out much! Nowadays I wander about in leggings, tatty tops and boots (most often wellies!) with an assortment of grubby coats, depending on the weather! As for makeup, a touch of tinted moisturiser and lip balm is about as good as it gets and that's only if I remember!

I was born and grew up in Plymouth and left to my mother, I would have been a vet or an RAF officer rather than what I went on to do. She couldn't quite grasp the idea that I was an average pupil who hated school and studying equally and wanted to escape my rather strict upbringing as soon as possible. As the youngest of six, with about thirteen years between me and the next of my siblings, the way I was raised was different to my peers. Mother was forty when I was born and having older parents meant their approach was more old fashioned than that of my school companions' parents. I went to an all-girls grammar school where expectations for achievement were high and we were, to a certain extent, expected to "fly the flag" for the future of successful women. While my contemporaries were out doing things like going into town at the weekends and going to discos after school, I had to study and help in the house. It made school life difficult sometimes, always being the odd one out and I hated my school days with a passion.

I was expected to be the "golden child," my siblings thought I was spoiled (in some ways I probably was, compared to them) and my mother frequently reminded me how much she did for me and how ungrateful I was, the price for being spoiled was emotionally high. I felt under constant pressure to do well and that no matter how well I did do, it was never good enough, a feeling I often experience to this day. Thankfully, my dad was a quiet, calming influence for me through my traumatic teenage years, when, like most people that age, I felt the world was against me and no-one cared.

My reaction to my mother's controlling nature was to walk out of grammar school in 1979, mid sixth form, in a fit of bravery (and probably stupidity), to train as a riding instructor at a yard on the edge of Dartmoor. Her reaction was, unsurprisingly, not good and after many arguments, I was left paying her half of my £25 a week wage for "rent" and walking three miles to catch the bus to work each day. The idea was to put me off so that I would go back to sixth form, but I was a stubborn mare and doggedly got on with it, whatever the weather, no matter how tired I was. It's funny, the lengths you'll go to as a rebellious teenager and horses are still a large part of my life, although that's a story for a different time.

Those lengths also included getting married to a Royal Marine at eighteen, against all advice, of course, as I knew best. This made working with horses difficult and I had to leave the stables and get a better paid job, ending up working for Marks and Spencer for a while before I had my son at the age of twenty.

During the eighties, just as now, people were having to work hard to keep their jobs in difficult economic and social times. It was still archaic in the workplace for women and wages were definitely unequal, we were faking it till we made it, an expression that definitely wasn't invented by the Millennials!

I had managed to get a job with a well-known Optician's at the time and was lucky enough to be put forward for a new role as part of a national team of Computer Systems Trainers. After various internal interviews, I managed to secure one of the available positions in the South West and enjoyed the job immensely, learning many skills that have come in useful since. This was at a time when not many offices had computer systems, let alone in the retail side of optics and if memory serves me right, the company

I worked for was one of the first to install computers in their branches.

I travelled throughout the South West, installing the systems and training the staff, meeting new people and staying in nice hotels. The computer systems we were using were nothing like the laptops and tablets of today, they were cumbersome machines with large, bulky monitors that took up a great deal of desk space and there was certainly no sign of Microsoft Windows! Gaming consoles were nowhere in sight, gaming was something people did on a machine in the pub, playing at shooting down aliens, if the pub was modern enough!

I remember being sent to Redruth in Cornwall to install their new computer system and train the staff. Arriving quite late at the hotel where I was to stay for the week, I was surprised to see it in darkness. I tentatively knocked on the door and eventually a lady opened it to greet me. I explained who I was and it was then that she told me I couldn't possibly be booked in as they didn't open in the winter! She took pity on me and kindly let me in, then went to check the booking register, only to find that someone had made a mistake with diary and told our office that the booking was fine! I have never forgotten how kind the owners were, they opened a room for me, went out to get me a takeaway for supper and set me up with coffee-making supplies. The next morning, they even made me some breakfast and told me that they were happy for me to stay the week, despite being officially closed and I enjoyed the rest of the stay there, feeling very welcome, despite the booking error.

After a couple of years, once all the systems were installed and people trained, I went back to my original role but couldn't settle back into static life. The combination of this and my husband's military service told on our marriage and we split up around the same time, so, after a chat with the personnel department at work, I became mobile again, covering short staffing, holidays and sickness in branches around the region. I moved to Somerset as my base because it seemed like a good idea at the time. It wasn't and I spent many years regretting the decision (and several others!) to totally uproot myself and my son. I wasn't really enjoying my job anymore either and it was difficult to find childcare without my family nearby, so I found an IT administrator's job locally. I can't honestly say I enjoyed that job either, nor many of the roles I took over the subsequent years, they were neither exciting nor interesting by any means, just a source of necessary income.

I eventually started work as a Senior Service Controller for an emergency alarm company, the sort that deals with alarm pendants and door entry systems for the vulnerable. That wasn't a bad job and we had some fun until they closed the regional offices down and I was job hunting again, with a very small redundancy payment to manage with in the meantime.

I went back to doing temporary work for an agency to keep us going and eventually got a job as a Year 2000 Project Coordinator - remember Y2K, with the Millennium bug and everything being expected to grind to a halt because the date system on all computers stopped at 1999? It was my job to work on contingency planning for a housing association in case that did happen and instead of seeing in the new Millennium at a party, I had to stay near a phone without a celebratory drink, just in case I was needed. As we all know, the world didn't come to an end and I wasn't needed, oh well, at least I was paid extra!

My contract was set to end in January of 2000, so I was job hunting yet again. Jobs in my line of work were in short supply in the area and in a somewhat rash moment, I agreed to go back to working with horses at a friend's event yard. It was enjoyable to start with, but I realised it wasn't for me anymore. I was getting too old to be a glorified groom, working long hours and having no energy left to do anything with my own horses, let alone have a social life. I had never been an eventer nor had the desire to become one, with showing and show jumping being my game, so eventually I moved on, taking a few part time jobs and working for a temping agency again to keep money coming in.

I was getting tired of my temping work when an opportunity to rent my own stud and livery yard came up, something I had always wanted to do, so the horses and I moved and soon afterwards I met my partner, Jon, who farmed next door and supplied my hay.

We eventually started seeing each other and he asked me to move in with him at the farm. I wasn't terribly keen on the idea as I preferred living on my own and was fresh out of a relationship anyway. I said I would think about it but was actually trying to find a way around it until I was happier with the idea, however, things were getting difficult on the yard as my ex was still there with his horse, which made things terribly awkward and there were problems looming on the horizon with the landlord as business began to slow down, making the rental payments a struggle. Knowing the problems I was having made Jon more determined to persuade me to make the move. Eventually and somewhat uncomfortably, I agreed, although with many reservations as he lived with his mum and I'd visited the house on a few occasions, not liking it at all. I didn't feel right there, the house never felt welcoming and it was like stepping back into a cross between Miss Haversham's bedroom without the wedding paraphernalia and a rag and bone man's storage shed, hoarder's heaven - my Hell! To make matters worse, it's probably the coldest and dustiest house I have ever lived in, the original part of it being over two hundred years old, I believe.

The house had been split into two on the death of Jon's father many years earlier and his sister and her family lived in one part while Jon and his mother lived in the other. Looking back, I know I was still uneasy about the move, that feeling made worse when I discovered that one of his relatives was against the whole idea. They felt that there wasn't room in his mum's part of the house for someone else and that she, his mother, already had enough to do looking after Jon!

I was indignant, I neither needed nor expected to be taken care of by an elderly lady, I was quite capable of looking after myself, as I'd always done. Unfortunately, I didn't feel I could back down from the move, so I spent the next several years feeling like a visitor, avoiding being in the way or being any sort of drain on the family life, buying my own food separately, cooking my own meals and generally staying out of the way. Any offers of help from me were brushed aside by his mother, not unkindly, but still leaving me feeling a nuisance. It wasn't an easy way to live and of course, I kept my feelings about the situation hidden from Jon, who never realised that there was a problem. I'm still not entirely comfortable, although I do have a good relationship with the ghost, who, in between leaving taps running and moving things to unlikely places, often opens and closes doors for me!

Meanwhile, circumstances at the yard weren't improving and eventually it was time to give up the stables and move on with the horses. There was nowhere suitable locally and I ended up having to take them onto a farm about five miles away as there was no room for the horses on Jon's land. There was at least one good thing about this move, the only one in fact, because it was there that I came back into contact with sheep, having already had some experience with them where I had kept the horses when I first came to Somerset.

CHAPTER 2

AND SO TO SHEEP

Curiously, it was horses that led me to my first hands-on experience with sheep. When I moved to Somerset from Plymouth, I had brought my elderly horse with me and kept him on a local farm for a while until he passed at the ripe old age of twenty six. A few years later, with three new horses and the need for somewhere nearby to keep them, I contacted the farmer where I had kept my first horse to ask if he knew of anywhere. As luck would have it, he pointed me in the direction of his neighbour's farm, so I got in touch and found he was willing to have us there.

I had always liked sheep and enjoyed seeing them on our day trips to various parts of Dartmoor when I was young and again whilst I was training to be a riding instructor on the edge of the moor, so I was delighted that the farm had mixed livestock and there were plenty of sheep for me to see.

One lambing season, due to his wife's pregnancy, the farmer found himself alone to do all the maternity work (not including his wife's!), along with everything else. Knowing I was fond of sheep and had often quizzed him about them, he asked me if I would mind taking on the night shift to check the ewes every couple of hours in return for hay and straw for the horses and an education in sheep, all I needed to do was wake him if there were any problems. I didn't need asking twice, I jumped at the chance and learnt a great deal that season and then again the following year.

His management system worked well, he would let the ewes out into the fields next to the shed to graze in the daytime and then call them in again in the evening by shaking a feed bag. They were very obliging, rarely keeping us waiting, like most sheep they would do anything for a feed! I spent the late winter nights sitting by the warmth of the Aga in the low-lit kitchen, reading and enjoying cups of delicious hot chocolate, going out to inspect the sheep for signs of imminent birth every couple of hours. There was a comforting warmth and a peaceful atmosphere in the shed, with the ewes quietly resting and chewing the cud, the occasional bleat and the joy of seeing the newly born lambs cuddling up to their mums and an even more comforting warmth going back in to sit by the Aga!

It was some years later that I came into contact with sheep again, which was after I had taken the horses to a new farm. As I got to know my new landlord, I was able to help out with his flock now and again, with worming, hoof trimming and such like. I started to feel that I had gained some knowledge and at the same time, a possible new vocation!

This new farm was some five miles away from home and for various reasons I had to walk there and back each morning, thankfully I had a lift for the evening trip. Even though it was keeping me fit, all that walking was putting a strain on my old body, as well as using up a good deal of time, so I needed to find a better way to make the journey. After listening to me complaining yet again, Jon leapt into action and decided fixing up onc of the many push bikes about the place was the thing to make my life easier. Ha, how wrong he was, did he but know it!

He dragged an old peppermint green and lilac bike from amongst the nettles, straightened the back wheel and gave it a back brake (shame there was no front one). Then he oiled, poked, prodded and finally produced a rideable, not too bad looking vehicle, apart from the garish colour, that is. Rideable, that is, by anyone who is not a forty seven year old (as I was at the time) with the balance of a one legged barstool.

My excitement and enthusiasm knew no bounds. Maybe that's a slight exaggeration, I was so thrilled at the thought of taking to the road on a couple of pieces of three inch rubber I would rather have pulled out my own teeth. Still, teeth intact and with my Jack Russell terrier, Bracken, in tow, I set out early one morning to ride about the yard a bit to get the feel of the bicycle.

Well, I must say that I don't think poor Bracken was ever the same again. He was a little concerned when I extricated the odd-coloured peril from the garage, even more alarmed when I climbed on board, feet barely reaching the ground and finally made a run for it when I wobbled perilously forward for all of two feet before having a nervous breakdown.

Not to be beaten by a vile coloured lump of metal, I called poor Bracken back from his hiding place and tried again. Poor dog, he couldn't believe how unlucky a JRT could be – what was the woman playing at, cursing at this wobbling thing - off he went again as fast as his legs could carry him amidst my cries of , "why can't I carry on walking" and "I can cope with walking each day!", which in reality, I couldn't. Jon had gone to a lot of trouble to help me so I had to try and ride the Beastly Thing, as it was quickly christened. I just hoped he didn't help again, well not with bikcs anyway.

The thing just kept wobbling, going off at tangents and refusing to stop when begged.

I decided to give it up as a bad job, went back in, told Jon it was unmanageable and set off on the walk to the horses – all this by quarter past six in the morning! I thought about the accursed bike as the day went on, kids ride them, elderly folks do, in fact everyone but me could ride a bike. Well, I wasn't having that. When I got back home I told Jon that I thought the seat was too high and the handlebars too low. See, ten minutes riding a bike badly and I was an expert, unfortunately, that did actually pretty much solve the problem, or so it seemed.

The intrepid Bracken and I set out next morning and as soon as I went to the garage the dog legged it, he wasn't taking any chances after the day before! I climbed aboard, wiggled myself into position and away I went, not so straight at the barn. Who was it said they couldn't hit a barn door? All they needed was a bike!

Despite the minor error, I tried again, got going and yelled to Bracken that I'd done it, just before teetering so much I nearly fell off. Bracken wasn't convinced, he waited until I put the bike away before coming anywhere near me, I had always said he was intelligent. That was it then, having made progress on the Beastly Thing I was going to have to venture onto the road.

Early the following morning I dragged the bike from the garage and headed for the open road. Wobble, bump, wobble some more and I managed to travel at least three yards at more than walking speed. The first hazard was to turn down the lane leading to the road across the local moor – memories of my brother's lessons on riding a bike as a child haunted me the whole way. He had taken me to the top of a steep local hill, told me he would hold on to the seat while I pedalled and then didn't! I survived the experience but I think the initial fear scarred me for life and I was reminded of it all these years later as the thing took on a life of its own and pelted down the lane hitting every hole and drain cover it could find.

When it reached the junction at the bottom, I prayed nothing was coming as the thing was completely out of my control and had shown further signs of having independent abilities. Remember that film about the murderous doll? Yep, the peppermint and lilac horror was the bike equivalent! I managed to wrestle it across the junction and round the next turn to the moor road.

Not too bad, I thought, a bit shaky still and quite bumpy because steering wasn't easy with the handlebars in a vice-like grip and my breathing a thing of the past. My legs weren't over-keen on the pedalling thing either and as I tried to master the incline to the railway bridge they took voluntary retirement. More wobbling and a gymnastic leap using the semi-retired legs in a way not normally humanly possible got me to the ground on both feet and I reached the bridge pushing the accursed bike. The temptation to sling it over the side was overwhelming, but the thought of injuring some innocent train driver stopped me and I climbed back on it. Of course, it was downhill again, so off it went like a wild thing, resisting all attempts to slow it down with its single brake. At this point I realised that my brother's teaching wasn't all in vain, I had a history of hanging on for grim death whilst being propelled downhill at speed! The road levelled out and I was about half way there - brilliant still alive and on board so far.

I set off on the long straight lane ahead of me and started to think this wasn't such a bad idea. The sun was shining, there was a gentle breeze, the birds were singing and then I had to brace myself to meet my first car as a cyclist. The bike suddenly had a fit of the vapours and pointed itself determinedly at the oncoming vehicle, despite all my efforts to force it into submission, then at the last minute it turned itself towards the ditch and finally gave in to the pressure of its only brake and stopped on a dangerous angle. I'm certain the car driver was never the same again, I thought he was going to die laughing.

Somewhat shaken, but not stirred, I grabbed it and forced it back onto the road. The next car came from behind and I nearly ended up in the ditch from the slipstream. Why do drivers think cyclists can ride in fairly straight lines at the edge of potholed lanes? Well, I guess most of them can, but these drivers should take into account people on uncontrollable, wild peppermint and lilac demon-possessed beasts.

I carried on regardless of my, or anyone else's, safety for that matter, until I reached the end of the moor and approached the main road between villages. At this point discretion (and self-preservation) became the greater part of valour and I dismounted with much relief. That will be easier, I thought and set off on foot. The Beastly Thing thought otherwise, it would not allow itself to be pushed in a straight line and resisted any pressure to bounce it up kerb stones. The retaliation was swift and sure, a quick pedal to the back of the calf had me calling on my Anglo Saxon dictionary and left me with a shiny bruise to display. Still, I limped onward and propped it up against a gate for a breather. Then came the piece de resistance, it threw itself hysterically to the ground, hitting me squarely in the ankle with its wheel and I hissed yet more Anglo Saxon at the beast! Thankfully my torture ended there for the day, I called home when I finished the horses and Jon took pity and offered to pick me and it up in the Land Rover, although I would have happily left it behind and there was still the next morning to look forward to.

My return to bike riding raised several questions. How do the folk on those skinny wheeled racing bikes manage to go so fast without hitting passing cars or landing in ditches? Do some drivers have to pass so close? How do racing bike folk manage to casually unfasten their drinks bottle and swig a great mouthful of liquid without a single wobble? Why do drain covers appear to move in front of the bike when you think you've missed them? For me, the biggest question of all – why do people ride bikes for pleasure?

A while later, I graduated to an electric tricycle, so much better for me and everyone else in the area!

CHAPTER 3

KEEPING SHEEP

Down at the yard, the sheep used to come into the sheds alongside the stables to lamb each season and one year, a tiny ram lamb kept escaping through the gate of his pen onto the yard. He would come out and wander around doing lamb stuff and watching what I was up to, but staying well away from any contact. One morning, while I was opening a round bale of hay for the horses, he walked straight up next to me and started nibbling on it. From that day on he was never very far away while I was working, becoming tamer every day and even enjoying a bit of fuss. I tried to put the thought of his destiny of going to market out of my mind and not get too attached, but that was just impossible as he was such a little character. Then I had the bright idea that I should try and persuade the farmer to let me buy him. It took him a while to agree, but he did give in, that's what happens when you get nagged every day! The only snag with it was that I hadn't mentioned anything to Jon about having a sheep. Never mind, I thought, I'll sort it out. I also needed to take into account that sheep are flock animals and to keep one on its own wouldn't have been fair, so I had to think about getting another.

As luck would have it, in the same shed that Lambie (as he became known) lived in was a slightly older orphan lamb who had mobility problems and frequently got knocked over. The poor little soul got pushed into the feed trough one day and was stuck fast so I went in to rescue him. I was carefully moving him around, chatting to him to try and keep him calm, when a voice behind me said "you might as well have that one too, it's only going to end up in the freezer anyway." Well, I couldn't say no could I? Now I had to persuade Jon to have two sheep on the farm (along with the various ducks, chickens, quail and guinea fowl that I had collected!). He is a cattle and arable farmer, as well as an agricultural contractor and sheep most definitely weren't on his list of things to add to the farm, in fact, he always said he would never have sheep. You know what they say though, never say never, so now I found myself in the situation where I had got two lambs and had yet to tell Jon before it would be time for them to come home.

Of course, it didn't end there, sheep are addictive in my opinion. Two black ewe lambs arrived on the scene, minus a mum, so naturally I had to find out more about them. I was told that they had belonged to someone who hadn't been able to keep them and so they joined the farmer's flock. I got to know them over a few days and knowing what their future was likely to be, it was time to start nagging the farmer yet again about having them. To shut me up, he said he would think about it. Clearly, they would be worth more at the market as finished lambs than sold to me at that point and it took a bit of time, but I can be very persuasive, well, persistently annoying then. I wore him down and added two more lambs to the collection. That meant there were four that Jon didn't know about!

Time moved on, as it does, so I needed to broach the subject with him. We had a chat about Lambie and it wasn't too difficult to persuade him to let me have him, which was a good thing really as the deal was already done. Then I started the line "but he can't live on his own" and got him to agree to Cutlet coming along too. I know that was a strange name as he was never in danger of being eaten, but it was a slightly amusing reference to the farmer's original freezer comment. Having managed to get an agreement for the two to come to the farm, I thought it might be best not to mention the black lambs for now, but wait a few days. I lost my nerve a bit and the few days extended to a couple of weeks and I still hadn't mentioned them when the day came to pick them all up.

I had no idea what I was going to do so though I would just wing it a bit. We loaded Lambie and Cutlet and then I just happened to say we needed to go to the other shed to pick up the girls. "What girls?" he said. "Oh, I thought I'd asked you about them, I must have had a senior moment," said the not so innocent me. I think he was so taken aback that he didn't know what else to do but drive up to the other shed and load them up. I must confess I have used a similar technique to this a few more times over the years but I don't think it will work forever! Anyway, so began my adventures into being a shepherdess!

My first year of sheep keeping was pretty uneventful, albeit a steep learning curve, but I did gain a good deal of experience in their care. Helping someone else with lambing is one thing, keeping your own flock, no matter how small, is something else entirely, with the sole responsibility for their welfare completely down to you. I had to learn more about foot trimming, shearing, worming, common ailments and everything was so different to all my experiences with horses.

Cutlet's mobility issues didn't improve but that just meant taking extra care of him, helping him out of his shed in the mornings and into the field just outside so that he could take short walks when he felt up to it, eat grass and generally do sheep stuff. At night and in bad weather I would help him back into the shed where he would happily eat hay with Lambie, who could come and go as he pleased but who chose to stay with his friend to keep him company. I would go out late at night to make sure he didn't need anything and it got me into the habit of going round the farm late at night to check on him, the other sheep and to make sure the poultry pens were secure. It's something I still do today, giving all the sheep a little piece of biscuit each at the same time.

Things got bit more exciting the following year with the arrival of my first home bred lambs. I knew the girls were pregnant, obviously, but wasn't absolutely sure when they were due to lamb, so I was excited early one morning to find Blackie giving birth to the second of twins in their field shelter. They were beautiful jet black boys, soon to be called Sooty and Sweep, who grew into big strong rams. A few days later Babs produced lovely white twins, a ewe and a ram, Sugar and Spice, who also grew into big, strong sheep. I say big sheep because I'm sure I've seen smaller Shetland ponies!

One of the things to watch out for with sheep as the warmer weather approaches is fly strike, the term given to the presence of blowfly maggots deep in the fleece which have started to attack the skin. The blowfly lays eggs in the fleece and the maggots hatch, sometimes within hours. They migrate down to the skin and start the damage. It's a horrible thing for the sheep and needs to be dealt with as a matter of urgency. There are various chemicals on the market that can help prevent strike but I prefer not to routinely use chemicals on my animals, only when really necessary and besides, using them doesn't guarantee that it won't happen anyway, application and the weather can affect the results. It isn't really possible to manage parasite control in large, commercial sized flocks in the same way as I do in my small flock, there wouldn't be enough hours in the day and this is where the proprietary products come into their own.

I learned about fly strike the hard way early on in my shepherding career when one day, I noticed that Babs was very quiet and not interested in her food, which was very unusual. I got hold of her and checked her for injury or signs of illness. Nothing seemed obvious, so I started to look deeper into her fleece and to my horror, I came across a large area of fly strike. I was mortified, I checked them every day for fly eggs and newly hatched maggots but clearly I had missed them. Filled with guilt and a touch of panic, I rushed off to find Jon for help. Not being a sheep man but being much more calm about the situation, he called a neighbouring shepherd who was kind enough to come straight round, armed with his shears and something to kill the maggots. I will forever be grateful to him for that mercy dash and for teaching me all about strike and early signs to look out for in the sheep in case eggs or maggots weren't obvious.

I thought we were out of the woods then but shortly afterwards Babs collapsed and couldn't get up. The vet felt that it was some kind of shock as nothing else was obvious, so she gave her some painkillers and antibiotics and said wait and see. The next couple of weeks were spent giving her syringes of flat, diluted, energy drink, really meant for people, every few hours, alternated with water to keep her hydrated. She just lay there on her side with a glazed look and had to be turned regularly to stop her getting sores. The vet had no suggestions and local sheep farming friends shook their heads and told me to cull her. I just felt sure that she was going to make it so I didn't give in and slowly she started to respond. Eventually she was able to get on to her front, with a couple of hay bales to prop her up and started to show an interest in nibbling a few ivy leaves, picked especially for her and some of the hay. A few days later Jon told me that he was certain that he had seen

Babs trying to stand up but I was sure he was imagining it, after all, she was always in the same position each time I went out to see to her. I did go out with him to check but she was still lying down, propped against a bale showing no signs of getting up and I thought he must have made a mistake.

Every few days we would move her pen to keep her on fresh grass and the next time we went to do it, as we lifted it, she shot across the field like a greyhound out of a trap and stuck her head down eating grass, leaving me standing there gaping like a goldfish! I couldn't believe my eyes, she had shown no sign at all that she could get up, letting me change her position regularly and enjoying all the treats that she was getting, crafty devil. The episode did leave her with contracted tendons which stops her straightening her front legs completely but she still manages well and can certainly run as fast as the others when she knows I want her for something. Babs is a really tough cookie and she proved it again a few years later, fighting for her life, and winning, again.

After the sudden heart breaking loss of Cutlet sometime later, Lambie and I were left devastated and he was incredibly lonely at the loss of his friend. I realised that, although nothing could replace Cutlet for me, Lambie needed the company of another sheep. I couldn't put him with the ewes and lambs, I didn't want to breed any more at that time, so I needed to consider another sheep (or two!). I had come across Herdwick sheep on the internet and thought they looked marvellous, so I did quick post on social media, asking if anyone in Somerset had any available. I couldn't believe my luck when a breeder not too far away contacted me. Cutting a long story short, Jon had agreed to one more but I had arranged to collect two wether lambs. I had to find a way to tell my long-suffering partner that I had bought two more sheep, not one.

There was a pattern emerging here, I had talked him into the first two sheep because they needed company and then added two more, here I was, going down the same route, to add another two to the collection. I did feel that this time I had better mention the subject a few days before we were due to pick them up though. "You know we're going off to Taunton to collect the sheep in a few days," I said. Jon gave me a suspicious look, he had guessed what was coming. "Well, I was thinking that rather than finding myself in the same situation again if something awful happens, maybe I should get two. They're really reasonably priced for Herdwicks too." Good soul that he is, Jon gave in but said no more sheep after the Herdwicks. "You'd better give the owners a ring to make sure they have another one available," poor chap, he had no idea that I had already done the deal.

On the day we were due to fetch them, I was ridiculously excited to get going, rushing all the chores and getting the trailer hitched up to the Discovery. We set off and joined the M5 heading south towards Taunton. All was well when, about halfway there, we caught a sudden smell of burning. Checking in the mirror, we saw that there were sparks and smoke shooting out behind us like something from a rocket on a launch pad. I had a minor panic attack while we headed for the hard shoulder and on checking under the bonnet when it was safe, Jon discovered that one of the pistons had melted so we wouldn't be going any further that day. I was so disappointed that I wouldn't be able to collect my sheep, I called the breeder to explain and arrange another visit. I don't think Jon saw that as the priority issue but hey ho, we're all different! What followed was a bone-chilling two hours on the edge of the motorway with a none-too happy Jon, waiting for a recovery truck to arrive. The whole escapade took hours longer than it should have and the reasonably priced sheep were not going to be so reasonable after all. The recovery cost nearly two hundred pounds, plus the fuel and the up-coming cost to make the trip again the following week. Added to that, we were cold, tired and hungry and still had work to do at the farm. We did manage to collect the boys the following week without further incident, luckily for me, because if we had broken down again, I think Jon would have left me by the motorway. To me, the whole thing was worthwhile because Herdy and Buddy arrived and moved into the paddock next to Lambie, who alternated between being interested and annoyed with the newcomers. I, on the other hand, was thrilled to bits with them and stayed that way. It was interesting to see how the colour of their fleece changed each year as they grew from the little dark clouds with white faces through to the easily recognised grey with white face and legs, gradually getting lighter as the years went by and they have the greatest characters ever.

CHAPTER 4

NAUGHTY BOYS AND GIRLS

I hadn't intended breeding any more lambs but Blackie was a bit of a devil for the boys and so it was no surprise to find a couple of years later, that she had managed to get in with one of the rams and the inevitable happened. What was done was done, so I waited for the arrival of the babies with cautious excitement. She did everyone proud by easily and safely delivering a set of triplets, two white and one black, which swelled the numbers of my slowly growing flock to twelve at the time, not bad considering I was only ever supposed to have two!

Blackie was always an awkward sort and was no different on this occasion. She decided there was no way she was having anything to do with the two white lambs, as far as she was concerned they were nothing to do with her, she'd had black ones before and had a black one now, so no way was she taking care of them. A trip to the local agricultural store for milk powder, bottles plus a heat lamp and there I was nursing two not-really orphan lambs while Blackie took care of the third – maybe she wasn't so daft after all! A bit of strategic pen building later and the two little white lambs were settled comfortably under the heat lamp, next door to their mum and brother. The theory was that I would supervise her with them all together a few times a day, whilst bottle feeding them both, until she accepted them. Blackie's theory was entirely different, they could go in with her and little Treacle for a bit but then she wanted them gone again. Needless to say, that while the lambs got on fine, Blackie was not going to feed them and that was that. Once the lambs were stronger and the weather a bit warmer, they were all able to go out in the paddock together, to anyone watching, a happy little family. The reality was that I still had to keep feeding Siggy and Tristan until they were weaned! It didn't do them any harm, though, as they are all big boys and at the time of writing five years old, although their mum has now sadly passed.

A bit later on in the year, Spice decided it would be a fabulous idea to break through the hedge and fence to join the large flock of sheep on the farm next door. I was horrified when I discovered what he'd done. I had no idea how I was going to get him separated and back home from a flock of about two hundred sheep, ewes of course and him being a ram! Time to phone my long suffering neighbour, the same one who rescued Babs from fly strike and confess that my ram was busy doing what rams and ewes do! Thankfully, he found the situation amusing, unlike me, and was happy to let him stay there, not least because he was a pretty decent type of sheep and although they already had a ram running with the ewes, there were plenty of ladies for them to share safely. The plan was that I would collect him next time they gathered the flock for worming and foot trimming. Spice, meanwhile, thought all his birthdays had come at once and wasn't in the least bothered with any plans that I was hatching with the ewes' owner.

Although I agreed Spice should stay where he was for the time being, I wasn't really happy with the idea as I prefer to take care of my own animals, after all, no-one does it the way you do. I would go round to check on him each day, but could never really get close enough other than to see that he was the right way up and apparently well. The rest of the flock didn't know me, so bolted across two huge fields as soon as I got near and he would go with them. All was well until one morning, while feeding my other sheep, I glanced over the hedge and was surprised to see Spice lying down on his own, not another sheep in sight. That is a red light to any shepherd, a sheep on its own like that is usually in some kind of trouble and so I immediately went round to see what was wrong. He was certainly in trouble, my poor boy was almost blind with an eye infection and thoroughly miserable. I was so upset, the flock was fed everyday but no-one had spotted anything, or if they had, they hadn't told me. In reality, it probably would have been difficult to spot in such a large flock, but I still felt aggrieved. We went back with the trailer to collect him and called the vet who dosed him up with antibiotics, painkillers and left some eye ointment to be used several times a day. The poor chap was so hungry and terribly dehydrated, struggling to find the water bucket because he had so little vision. I made sure he was drinking by holding his bucket to him every couple of hours and put his hay and feed right in front of him. On one visit, the poor soul was collapsed on the ground, gasping. The vet came as soon as I called and was with us very quickly, diagnosing pneumonia. It was touch and go for a few days, he was so ill, but he soon began to feel better and made a full recovery, including his eyesight, much to everyone's relief. You would think he would have learned his lesson but boys will be boys and he did it again the following year from a different field. This time he was only allowed to stay for a couple of days until we all had time to round up the flock and retrieve him, I wasn't going to risk that happening again.

Rams can be difficult and dangerous animals, not for the faint hearted or inexperienced for sure. It took me a little while and a few very painful experiences to learn never to turn my back or drop my guard when in with them, no matter how kind they pretend to be - there's no such thing as a sweet ram, not all of the time, anyway. My boys have taken pleasure in butting me head first into a wall, face-planting me in the mud, crushing my hand between horns and gate, leaving it bruised, battered and un-useable for a few hours, not to mention various bruises to my legs. I know I have been lucky in escaping serious injury, I have learned my lesson, a big ram is quite capable of breaking bones and I'm much more careful than when I started out, so I can say I have gained something from the various injuries!

CHAPTER 5

LIVING WITH CATTLE

Cattle – I have a sort of love, hate relationship with cattle. I mean, I love them but I hate getting involved in managing them, apart from maternity or nursing duties, both of which I have an inbuilt knack of carrying out in most animals. I only ever get involved in everyday work with them if there is no-one else to help. Ironically, it's not because I'm intimidated by them, it's more because they are not in the least in awe of me, they find me very amusing, in fact!

Take situations where they would need to be moved from one place to another.

Generally, helpers would stand in places where the cows are likely to break away and then the herd would either follow Jon while he shook a bucket or feed bag or he and his cousin would herd them from behind. If I stood in a strategic place, they would completely ignore me if they chose, trotting straight past, despite me performing some sort of insane country dance, clutching a big stick and mimicking those shouts to cattle that only farmers can make! I've been yelled at so many times for "letting them get away" but they really are not intimidated by me in the least, though somehow, it was always my fault!

At one time, we had a small part of the herd grazing in one of the fields on the moor but a couple of them insisted on jumping the ditch onto neighbouring land. Retrieving them would involve going through several fields onto the road and herding them back to their own patch, which could be a long and difficult job, so Jon decided to put them in the trailer and move them elsewhere. He and his friend managed to load all except one, my favourite actually, Ruby, so they took the others and then hatched a plan involving about six people, including me, to herd her the half mile or so back to the farm along the moor road. Not as easy as it may sound, various ungated droves, driveways and a road junction stood between the field and the farm. We all set off early the next morning, dropping people in various places to stop Ruby taking her own route. I was to follow her with a neighbour driving his truck to partially block the road behind while I walked with her to keep her moving on towards home. Jon was going to drive along in front in the Land Rover he used to feed from so that she would follow him, in theory anyway. We must have got two thirds of the way back when we discovered that we had missed an open gateway. Of course, Ruby spotted it, took off at a trot with me in hot pursuit and shot straight into someone's garden! Yep, apparently that was my fault, because I was shouted at for not outrunning her! Jon jumped out of the Land Rover, went in after her and out she came, took one look at me blocking her return to the original field and true to form, ran straight past me, all the way back to where we started! Lots more shouting and arm waving followed and I set off on foot to retrieve her again. Our neighbour and I managed to get her back on track and past the offending gateway and Ruby trotted on ahead, followed by him in his truck, while I was still walking behind. They very soon disappeared out of sight and I kept heading for home on foot. Sometime later, I saw the neighbour's truck heading towards me on his way home. I had walked a fair distance by now and thankfully he stopped, and gave me a lift back to the farm. He thought someone had come back for me already but no, the cattle crew were all at home, drinking tea and chatting, they hadn't even noticed I wasn't back! So much for helping with the cattle, no wonder I avoid it if I can!

Another problem for me was the bull, he was a massive, grumpy devil who took great delight in standing on the opposite side of the fence, pawing the ground and tossing his head from side to side, making it quite clear that if I dared come in, I was for it. On one occasion, he turned on Jon's cousin, an experienced cattleman himself, and tossed him a good distance across the field. Thankfully, his cousin was only heavily bruised, bad enough in itself but it could have been so much worse. I had always been very wary of that bull and avoided going in with him as much as possible, however, sometimes I had to bite the bullet and do it.

A few weeks after that incident, one of those times arose. Another favourite of ours, Calfy, gave birth to a stillborn calf and couldn't get up. Jon was with her, waiting for the vet and I was at the farm waiting for news. The weather was beginning to take a turn for the worse with thick, dark clouds heading in and I knew that Jon had no waterproofs with him and there was nothing to protect Calfy from the elements either. Right, I thought, I'll grab some waterproofs and one of the horses' spare outdoor rugs and take them over to the field, several miles away. The only problem was, I had a broken ankle, so I enlisted the help of Jon's nephew and his fiancée who were visiting from Wales and we set off on our mission. They only had an ordinary saloon car and the ground was quite soft, so when we arrived, we had to park at the gate and walk across a field to reach the others in the orchard. I hobbled all the way there and we reached them just after the vet arrived whose first words to me were, "Should you be walking around fields with a broken ankle?" My safest response as I tried to ignore the throbbing pain was "no comment", certainly not what I was thinking!

Jon still had to deal with the other cattle after the vet had gone, so he and his nephew set off in the Land Rover to see to them on the other side of the road, leaving his nephew's fiancée and I in the orchard with Calfy. As soon as they were out of sight, from nowhere, appeared the bull. We were frozen to the spot, there was no-where for us to go and I wasn't in a position to carry out any nifty escapes anyway! We stared at him and he stared at us – waiting to hear the Landie engine felt like longest few minutes of our lives, I've never been so relieved to see that vehicle approaching. As soon as they reached us, the bull walked off and to this day I'm sure I heard him laughing! After all that, the threatening weather never came to anything either, not even a drop of rain fell, but at least Calfy recovered well.

Jon's farm is both cattle and arable farming and one of the legal requirements about keeping cattle is the need to have them TB tested regularly, as per the DEFRA/APHA regulations in the UK. The time frame between tests depends on the risk in the area the cattle are in, at the time of writing, usually bi-annually, annually or six monthly, with additional testing if there are any positive results in nearby herds. This involves a skin test (SICCT) where each cow is injected with two types of Tuberculin and then checked three days later to assess the skin reaction. This is a very simplistic description of the whole procedure but just about covers it.

The last thing you want to see by day three is a significant lump at the injection site – a positive result, called a reactor. There is only one end to that story, the loss of the animal and various restrictions and retesting over the next several months.

A few years ago, after farming cattle for over thirty years with no TB problems, Jon experienced his first reactors. Two of the cattle tested positive and so their end was signed and sealed. It was the most distressing time for all, the poor cows couldn't be taken away by Jon, we had to wait for someone designated by DEFRA to come and collect them. They had to be isolated from the rest of the herd and in our case, that meant they had to be kept at the home farm, so every time we went out to do anything, including looking after them obviously, we had to walk past them knowing what their fate was. It was so upsetting to see these two apparently healthy animals waiting for their fate, although I guess they didn't know. It was two weeks before they were collected and I was so upset the whole time, these two had been destined to stay with us, they were never going to be sold and Jon had bred one of them himself. It was just heart-breaking and Jon was very good, as he always is about things like this, he made sure that I wasn't around when they were collected and taken off to their ultimate end. I understand the need to keep the great British public safe but the test has been used for a long time and many times its efficiency has been called into question by the farming community. I don't know the science of it, I just wonder whether more research needs to be done. What made it all worse was that when the post mortem report came back, whilst one apparently had lesions, the other didn't. Having the reactors meant that the whole herd was put under movement restrictions, we had a visit and a list of questions from an APHA vet and the cattle retested twice at short intervals. It was a long period of anxiety whilst waiting for the final clear test and permission given to return to normal. The lead up to testing time (every six months in this area now, although it was annually then) was always worrying but since the TB breakdown, it became so much worse and still is today.

CHAPTER 6

GUINEA FOWL AND OTHER POULTRY

Of course, in my mind, no farm is complete without chickens. Since moving to the farm, I have kept various species of poultry, call ducks, Campbell cross ducks, chickens – both large and bantam - quail and guinea fowl.

Guinea fowl - those two words fill me with trepidation. Anyone who has kept guinea fowl will know exactly what I mean!

On the spur of the moment, despite having well over a hundred poultry of varying species, I decided to by two beautiful lavender pearl (a soft, pinky grey colour with tiny white spots) guinea keets (chicks) from a friend. She did warn me they could be noisy and they are! For the first few weeks they had a pen in the conservatory next to the kitchen. This made a nightmare of any time spent in there, they would get terribly excited and shout their two-tone call as loudly as possible for the whole time anyone was around. If you've never heard a guinea fowl, check out the internet, you'll never be the same again!

They do have another loud noise that they make, their alarm call. That is something else, imagine and old fashioned football rattle, the wooden ones that you would spin around in the air, then imagine it three times as loud and you'd be pretty close! It's very effective at warning the approach of predators or strangers but it does nothing for your nerves!

A couple of years later, Jon had asked me to think about what I would like for my birthday and having seen some guinea fowl for sale not too far away, I decided I'd like them. Why, I do not know, I was very happy with the girls I had, despite the noise they could make. They were outside by then, so a few more wouldn't hurt, would they?

Off we went to collect them, a pied male and two royal purple females and the fun started immediately. They had been confined to a shed to make it easier to catch them - trying to catch guinea fowl is on a par with holding water in a net - in fact, the only benefit to them being inside was that they couldn't disappear into the distance! After what seemed like forever, we got them into the poultry carrier amid the horrendous noise of their alarm calls and various escapes as we tried to put each one in, (they are large, nimble and evasive creatures that move like lightening). We drove them home and there

I learned all about semi-feral guineas in comparison to my relatively tame ones!

The girls weren't too bad, although very noisy but the male was a devil in disguise, he took every opportunity to scream his alarm call, escape and then sit just out of reach on the top of the big flights that he was meant to be inside of. Not that reaching him would have done any good, if you got within a foot of him he was off again, always at dusk, with me using a good deal of swear words, oaths and curses while I followed him around, trying to get him to ground level so I could herd him back in. He'd been told more than once that I could stop being vegetarian for a night and the oven was warm!

One evening he set off on another great escape mission and I spent what felt like forever trying to get him back in to stop him ending up as fox fodder. As darkness started to fall, he headed into a thick bramble hedge where there was no hope of reaching him in any way. I was just thinking that I would probably be one guinea fowl down by morning, when his face appeared at the window of the cab of one of the old tractors by the hedge, I took my chance and slammed shut the drop-down window at the back and he was trapped. My last sight of him by torchlight that night was his furious face at the window, full of annoyance as he'd been duped! I left him there for the night and rescued him in the morning when he was very happy to go back to his girlfriends and have some feed. He's called Dick, by the way, I'm sure you'll guess why!

When thinking about noisy poultry, there are few noisier than a female Call Duck. I used to have forty Calls then (down to twenty now) and all I needed to do was walk past them to set off an ear-shattering noise that was beyond description! They were developed from mallards to be a small, noisy decoy duck and have been in Britain since the mid-1800s. They would be tethered at the end of catch nets and their loud quacks would attract other ducks into the nets. These days, their small size and cute looks make them popular pets, although sometimes I wonder why I ever bred them – especially as I always keep what I breed! All it takes to shatter my nerves is a flock of screaming calls and alarmed guinea fowl, ear defenders have been a serious consideration more than once!

I've always found poultry-keeping quite straightforward but there have been a couple of individuals who I often described as challenging. One of those was a big white Orpington cockerel, Roger, who spent the whole of his life planning ways to attack me without warning. He would hide behind anything large enough and wait for me to walk past and then, without warning, he would launch himself into the back of my legs, his spurs usually leaving deep scratches in my calves, along with a good few bruises. Orpingtons are large birds and Roger must have weighed about five kilos. It doesn't sound heavy but it certainly felt it when propelled at speed, armed with spikes and in full-on attack! I'd find myself creeping about, trying to see around corners and not get caught unawares, it didn't always work though.

Another cockerel I had issues with was much smaller, he was a little hybrid bantam I bred called Gordon. He was only tiny but he took his role as the bantam flock guardian very seriously, no-one was going to get near his ladies, including me. His attacks were more random that Roger's and certainly a whole lot less painful but being suddenly launched at by a little dervish wearing feathers did nothing for my nerves. Nothing I did stopped him but as luck would have it, Gordon taught himself a lesson that cured him for life. I was walking past his group carrying a bucket of water when he decided it was random attack time. He threw himself at me, all feathers and claws, but completely misjudged his aim and landed straight in the bucket. I grabbed him out of the water to stop him drowning, getting soaked in the process and took him inside to dry him off before taking him back to his ladies. He never attacked me again, I'm not sure if it was gratitude for saving him or whether he thought I'd tried to kill him but at least I only had to worry about Roger getting me, shame he didn't land in a bucket, it may have worked on him too!

I only have fifty birds these days and the latest addition has been a pheasant! The stable cat wandered onto the yard and unceremoniously deposited a newly hatched pheasant chick on the floor. Not rating the chick's chances of survival, I took her home and put her in the brooder with a heat plate, sometimes called an electric hen, to snuggle under. Against the odds, she pulled through and at the time of writing, I share the office with a five month old feathered lunatic who takes great delight in dancing on the keyboard and clearing the desk every time I leave the room and who has her own group of followers on my social media blog! Until you have experienced life with an indoor pheasant (at least until the Spring when she can join the other birds), I can tell you that the best description would be an insomniac dervish who will suddenly take to the air without warning, clearing every conceivable surface she can before landing on the windowsill and preening her feathers as though she had nothing to do with the carnage surrounding her!

CHAPTER 7

SHEEP AND SHEARING

In late spring or early summer sheep need to have their fleece removed for their health and wellbeing – known as shearing. Contrary to the beliefs of some factions, sheep are not killed to be shorn, if they were, there wouldn't be any sheep!

There can be various problems if sheep don't get shorn, one of those being fly-strike, which can cause death quite quickly if left untreated. Whilst there are various commercial products to repel the flies, sheep can still be vulnerable and it's a horrible thing which needs prompt attention. There are various signs that a sheep has strike that experienced shepherds will spot early on, but, at the very least, shearing makes it easier to spot any danger sooner. Removing the wool makes it easier to see the overall condition of the animal too and imagine how heavy years and years of fleece growth would be to a sheep who is left without attention and what parasites might lurk beneath!

I confess to being really particular about who deals with my sheep and it took me a while to find a shearer who I was really comfortable with. My experiences with shearers were somewhat variable, they either turned up very late without calling to let me know and then rushing the job, scaring the sheep and cutting their skin in the process, or didn't arrive at all and then called late in the evening to see if tomorrow would be OK etc. It wasn't just the inconvenience of gathering them in early to be ready and then having to keep them in overnight because no-one turned up or rain was forecast and they couldn't be shorn if the fleece was wet, it was the fact that some shearers could be quite rough which annoyed me and although the job was done well enough, it was with little apparent care for the sheep. In the end, I learned how to hand shear the bigger sheep myself, nothing like a professional job but the wool comes off and the sheep are less stressed (me too!).

When the Ouessant sheep came along, I didn't feel confident enough to do the fast moving little folks safely so I went on the hunt for someone who could fit the bill. I consulted the ever useful (well, sometimes) social media for shearers and checked out comments on their work. A name that I kept seeing was Guy Old, along with glowing comments and not a bad word anywhere. He looked like the shearer for me so I got in touch and made an appointment.

Guy travels around the country on a pre-planned route that he organises in plenty of time, shearing small and large flocks and I waited with my usual edginess for the day to arrive.

I had nothing to worry about, he confirmed the night before, arrived on time and proved to be an experienced, skilled shearer (with many awards, incidentally) who was kind to the sheep, whilst doing a high class job. The bonus was that Guy brought his partner, Denise, to help and she is another lovely person who, by the way, makes gorgeous fudge, a serious weakness of mine when it comes to food!

From the outset, the shearing process left me with lots of fleece and no idea what to do with it. As it is such a fantastic natural, sustainable, eco-friendly, biodegradable resource, throwing it away didn't sit well with me and I headed for the internet for ideas. As always, there was a rich mine of useful information and quite frankly, some weird stuff too!

The first thing I needed to learn was how to prepare the raw fleece, washing and carding it, that is combing all the fibres to lie the same way, to make it ready to craft with. This sounds fairly straightforward, but it was nothing of the sort. Washing raw fleece by hand is an art in itself, a process of soaking and re-soaking several times in very hot water to remove the lanolin and a year's worth of whatever the sheep has managed to get into it, then repeating the process to rinse it. Through the whole wash, the water needs to be kept at a similar temperature and the fleece agitated as little as possible to prevent it becoming an un-useable felted mess! I did have a few disasters but got the hang of it in the end, although it's definitely my favourite thing to do.

The first craft I taught myself from online videos was needle felting. Needle felting is the art of taking a sharp, barbed needle and stabbing the wool into some kind of recognisable shape, whilst avoiding your fingers. I have failed in that department many times and it is so painful, a barbed needle forced at speed into yourself is definitely not to be recommended. There's a lot more to needle felting in reality but that's the basis of it.

The first thing I made was something that vaguely resembled a sheep, though it did have some conformational issues that wouldn't have won any prizes in a show! I still have that little sheep though, made from Cutlet's fleece. I persevered and with practice, my little home-made sheep improved enough for me to enter the craft competition held as part of the North Somerset Agricultural Society Ploughing Match for a bit of fun. I made two little felted Herdwicks from Herdy and Buddy's fleeces, one standing and one lying down. They took me a while to make but I didn't think they looked too bad for beginner and did resemble Herdwicks a bit.

The day of the match dawned and after seeing to the animals, we packed up Jon's entries for the hay and straw classes, three lots of my poultry eggs that were entered in the produce section, my very novice flower arrangement and two little felted sheep and set off.

The match is held in September each year and has classes for ploughing, hedge cutting, hedge laying, crops, produce, baking, crafting and lots more, a really nice autumn day out. The time of year means that more often than not, it's a cold, damp and windy day. I always feel the cold and that day was no exception, there was a strong wind with rain clouds lurking overhead. We were glad to get inside the marquee to set out the entries and have a coffee before heading back to the farm and the rest of the chores while waiting for the judging to be completed. We went back in the afternoon to see how our entries had fared but not really expecting much and to watch some of the ploughing, Jon's thing really but I enjoyed watching the heavy horses working, so it wasn't so bad. We discovered that our efforts had been well-rewarded, my felted sheep had won and the judge had left a note saying how much she liked them and our success continued with wins in the egg and flower arranging classes and good placings for Jon's hay and straw. The ploughing match became an annual event for us and we are lucky enough to be successful each time plus we enjoy looking at the all the other exhibits. People's creativity is amazing, there are some fantastic entries in all the sections, especially the baking. I love looking at all the lovely cakes that are entered. I couldn't make anything like them, mine would be more like biscuits. I have to imagine what the cakes taste like because I would put on weight if I so much as licked the fork!

My needle felting skills improved and I made many more things, showing them off on my social media accounts. I was surprised when I started to get requests from people to make items for them, especially from their own fleece and that encouraged me to start my small business, which began to grow steadily as I learned more about my craft. To keep people interested in my work, I decided to add other fleece crafts to my repertoire and another visit to the internet was called for.

I had always admired felted fleece rugs, also known as vegetarian sheepskins, which look like sheepskin rugs but actually are only made from the fleece, so there's no harm to the sheep. This idea fitted in perfectly with my ethos, so I watched some videos and after a series of failed attempts – nothing is ever as easy as it looks on the video - I finally got the hang of it and went on to make them regularly, specialising in my Ouessant fleeces, as they are really beautiful to work with and every one turns out differently. It is a long process involving laying out several crossing layers of carded fleece and laying on the long locks of a natural fleece before starting to add hot water, and soap, then using a rubbing and rolling technique7 to felt the cut ends of the locks into the backing fleece – a delicate process with no guarantee that the result will work.

From there, I went on to make peg loom rugs, felted insoles and orphan lamb coats, while still creating my wool animal sculptures that are much more refined than my first little sheep and I'm always on the lookout for new ideas to try.

As more people contacted me for commission pieces as well as my stock pieces, I realised that I that maybe I should stop treating my sort-of business as a hobby that made a bit of money and turn it into something credible. It was while I was learning about felting rugs that I came across an American lady called Amika Ryan of Shepherd Like A Girl and Copia Cove Icelandic Sheep and Wool, who is not only a shepherdess and talented crafter, but also a brilliant craft business mentor. I joined her social media groups and her free business workshops about starting and building a handmade craft business. Her advice, ideas and continued online support gave me the confidence to move from hobby business to a real business that has continued to grow with her ongoing guidance. Amika's guidance has made a huge difference to my confidence as a craft business owner and I would recommend her to anyone looking for help in that direction.

CHAPTER 8

THE WORST YEAR

I have often been told how lucky I am to live on a farm, what a wonderful way of life it must be and how much people would like my lifestyle. This usually comes from people who have seen the pretty version of life on a farm in some of the TV entertainment programmes, the reality is often very different. It can be lovely, when the animals are well, the weather good and there's enough money to pay the bills but it can also be a very different story. They wouldn't envy us the long hours, nor the days that we have lost animals despite our and the vets' best efforts, or when we're working in the pouring rain, gales, mud, snow and ice or wondering if we can afford to pay the bills and buy the animal feed. We don't have time to be ill, there's no-one to cover for us and if we get injured, well, bad luck, we have to work through it. I do consider myself very lucky to have the life I have but there are times when I wonder whether I can face going on with it all and the autumn of 2018 through to the late spring of 2019 was one of those times.

The saddest thing about keeping animals is that they don't live forever. Each time I've lost one of mine it's been like losing a little piece of me and I miss them for a long time, none are ever forgotten, but that year was the most awful I'd ever had with the animals.

It started with the loss of my oldest and favourite horse, Brook, at the age of thirty one. He had been with me for over twenty years and we had had a lot of fun together. I found him in the field one morning, clearly having passed peacefully as the ground showed no signs of disturbance. I suppose that was a small consolation but it didn't lessen the shock or grief. A couple of months went by and a freak accident resulted in the loss of Kris, a twenty five year old who I'd taken on after he had a bad racing injury sixteen or so years before. He was a gentle giant of a horse and I couldn't believe he had gone. The loss of Kris was followed just a couple of weeks later by Tim, also aged twenty five, who I had had from a yearling. He had to be put to sleep because of an old injury that he couldn't cope with any more. It was the only thing to do, he wasn't able to stand, but coming to terms with it was doubly hard. It was a dreadful time, I felt hurt and lonely in grief, I had taken care of them every single day for so many years and for them to not be there amongst the others was hard to accept.

Just as I felt Fate was going to leave me and my horses alone for a while, a lovely little twenty four year old pony succumbed to heart failure and I had to ask Lucy, our vet, to stop her suffering. Her name was Jade, but I had always called her Mary-Jane, no idea why, it just suited her and she was one of the nicest ponies I had ever met.

Still reeling from the loss of four horses in a short time, I really wasn't ready for what happened next. One of the rams had managed to get to Babs and Blackie one afternoon and of course, the inevitable happened. It wasn't too much of a problem, I didn't want to breed more lambs but I had the space and was able to care for them so didn't worry, not until a couple of weeks before Blackie was due to lamb that is. She became very quiet and disinterested in eating, so a visit from the vet was arranged. She was diagnosed with twin lamb disease, a condition where the ewe's system is struggling to maintain herself and her unborn lambs and so her nutritional energy levels need to be raised urgently. This can happen even when they have access to minerals and plenty of feed, as Blackie did. She was given a couple injections and I had to give her a special drench every couple of hours but despite all our efforts, she passed away. I was devastated and full of self-blame, with yet another loss to deal with.

By now I was totally paranoid about Bab's impending lambing, checking on her far more often than necessary but, as it turned out, it was a good thing I did, as late one night she suffered a vaginal prolapse. With my spirits at an all-time low by now, the vet was called again and I waited for him to arrive. Eventually, at about three in the morning, he materialised, replaced the prolapse and stitched it in place. The next day, Bab's shed was my first stop and to my horror, she had prolapsed again, despite the stitching. Another vet visit and everything was put back in place and re-stitched.

Breathing a sigh of relief and with everything metaphorically crossed, I got on with the usual jobs over the next few days, wondering when the next call to the vet would be. I didn't have to wait long, within a couple of days Babs was clearly unwell, so I reached for the phone again. Another of the vets came out to her and was shocked to find that she had gone down with a massive infection. What followed was weeks of treatment and emergency visits at various times of day and night by the most dedicated vet I know, Lucy Jones, who got Babs and I through all the trauma, including the loss of the unborn triplets due to the infection and then going above and beyond to successfully save my poor ewe. Lucy spent so much time at the farm that we joked it would be easier for her if I made up the spare room.

Surely, no more heartbreak I thought, I'd lost all these animals in a few months, it just wasn't fair but of course, Fate decided to throw me a grand finale and took Lambie from me without warning. He had been fine late the night before, munching his bedtime biscuit, having a fuss and just being himself and by the next morning he was gone, lying next to his fence, just like he was leaning on it, sleeping. I knew something was wrong as soon as I saw him, he didn't get up as I opened the gate and it was obvious then that my lovely, first-ever sheep had passed in the night. I was heartbroken for a long time afterwards and then, six months later, I lost my lovely Herdy because of bladder stones. At this point, I seriously wondered whether it was time to give up. I could only deal with a certain amount of sadness, my animals are important to me as individuals and yes, I do love them.

Outwardly I was coping with all the tragic events but inwardly I was a wreck. I felt responsible for everything that had happened. To me, if I had only done things differently, maybe managed things better, then at least some of those events wouldn't have happened.

Having suffered from bouts of depression since being a teenager, it wasn't long before I found myself in a dark place mentally, not being in control of anything, feeling a complete failure and with a sense of having let my animals down. I recognised the signs of the oncoming depression but dealing with it was something altogether different. I was extra tired, had no interest in anything, only doing what needed to be done, with extreme mood swings and a feeling of loneliness and helplessness. I turned on myself, not for the first time, feeling such a sense of self-loathing at my inability to do anything properly.

I still don't understand what made me focus on my diet, maybe it was the need to feel in control of something, but I decided that not only was I useless but I looked disgusting too. I consulted the internet to find out how many calories I should be having a day and then reduced that figure by three hundred. I cut out many of the foods I normally had and painstakingly wrote down everything I ate, along with the calorie total for each, to make sure I stayed within the magic number. I lost a lot of weight quite quickly, (I weighed myself daily), I was about nine and a half stone when I started and was heading towards eight stone very quickly.

Jon, knowing me so well, had realised that something was wrong, despite my outward act and suggested I went to see the doctor. I would have none of it but I did listen to what else he said and with his help and support became a little less obsessed with my food intake, although I was still writing everything down and checking my weight daily.

It's been a long road to recovery, but things are much better with the support from my long-suffering other half and I've stopped making a note of my calorie intake, although I'm still quite strict with what I actually eat.

Farming life is tough and we tend to suffer in silence, especially with mental health issues, so, when people tell me how wonderful it all is, I smile and agree and think to myself, not everything is as it seems, today maybe great, but tomorrow, who knows?

CHAPTER 9

COVID AND FRACTURES

In August 2020, whilst in the midst of the Corona virus pandemic, I decided it would be a really good time to have an accident, as if things weren't already difficult enough! Finishing up late night feeds for the horses, I stepped on a bit of loose hay on the concrete floor of the big shed. I hit the floor like a lump of lead, accompanied by the most horrendous cracking sound, just like someone breaking a branch. I stayed still for a moment and although I couldn't feel any pain, I knew for sure something was broken, I just didn't know what. My first thought was who was going to take care of my animals if I had to have an operation. I ust didn't know what I would do, Jon wouldn't be able to do everything.

Out on the yard, Jon was waiting in the truck for me to finish up but the problem was that he couldn't see me from where he was parked and I had stupidly left my mobile phone in the car. I tried shouting and hollering to no avail and after a couple of minutes, I thought I should try and get up. Well, that was hilarious, depending on your sense of humour, I discovered that while I could feel no pain while I was sitting down, getting up brought about a whole new level of agony and I was yet to get where Jon could hear or see me. Slowly, painfully and with much cussing, swearing and crying, I dragged myself to the front of the nearest stable and managed to stand up by leaning on the door. Now all I had to do was get to the front of the shed, not one of my best ideas, as I found out. I thought I was in pain when I first tried to stand up but it was nothing compared to what it felt like while I moved to the front of the shed (we're talking a full sized cattle shed here, not a field shelter size), with a combination of sliding and dragging myself along the front of the stable doors. I finally reached got there after what seemed like forever and I got to a place where Jon might hear me shouting. I started yelling like a banshee, still with no response, he was listening to the radio and reading a tractor magazine by torchlight. I got more and more hysterical with my shouts until eventually he heard me. He opened the car window, "What do you want now?" I shouted back "I think I've broken my ankle". His response was "What do you want me to do?" I can safely say that a few things crossed my mind at that point but I decided to go with "Can you feed the last horse and take me to hospital please," rather than some of the other things that were running through my mind!

We set off, first to the farm to let the dogs out and then on to the local emergency department, except that on the way, I remembered that it closed at ten pm and it was well after eleven by now. Jon was not impressed because we had to turn back and travel another twelve miles to the next nearest emergency department. Eventually we got to the hospital and I spent the next six hours waiting alone because of the covid virus, no-one but the staff and patients being allowed in. It was a miserable wait, I'd had nothing to eat or drink for hours, the porter had parked the wheelchair as far from any vending machines as possible and it was one of the type that had to be pushed by someone else, not so much of a problem, in fact, as in the furore I hadn't picked up my purse anyway. Jon collected me at about six the following morning and after a quick cup of coffee, I was outside by seven thirty, discovering the joys of trying to feed sheep and poultry, whilst being absolutely exhausted and dragging a painful ankle about in a fracture boot. I felt like a carthorse on cobbles and it was even more fun (not!) when I went on to the horses and one of them bumped into me, knocking me over because I couldn't keep my balance. I lay on the floor like a stranded whale, I couldn't get up but luckily a friend was with me and helped me up again. How I love animals, they're always so considerate!

Over the next couple of days one of Jon's friends came and helped me feed the sheep, which made a big difference and it was wasn't long before I was managing reasonably well, hobbling around with this ghastly boot on my leg that managed to knock itself into every conceivable object, sending a new wave of pain for me to deal with. After three weeks of this, I had had enough and decided to try to go without the boot for part of the day, it was a bit risky but luckily I healed fast and managed to dispense with the boot altogether. On my next visit to the hospital, the consultant was a bit surprised that I was bootless but agreed that I could carry on without it, providing I promised to wear yard boots that supported my ankle while I was working and for once in my life, I took the doctor's advice and did exactly that. I came out the other side of the whole affair with no lasting damage but a much more careful attitude to hay on concrete floors!

CHAPTER 10

OUESSANT SHEEP AND CRAFTING

My first contact with Ouessant sheep actually came through my craft business, little did I know where that initial encounter was going to lead me.

I received a message through my social media business page from a lady called Jo Jenkins (now March) who had just lost a very special old Ouessant ewe, Jazz, and was looking for a little memorial sculpture of her, made from her fleece. I was happy to oblige and in the course of our messaging, asked about Ouessants as I hadn't come across them before.

With Jo and the internet's help, I learned that they are the smallest, naturally occurring breed in the world, with ewes standing at about eighteen inches at the shoulder, the rams about nineteen and originating from the Isle of Ouessant off the coast of Brittany. They have a beautiful fleece in a variety of colours – black, white, brown in the breed standard but also a variety of other colours such as rusty mid-sides and Swiss. An average fleece weighs in at about one and half pounds and grows about three inches in a year, it is very versatile and can be used for a variety of crafts, from spinning to felting and pretty much everything in between. It also has all the attributes of other fleece, being natural, sustainable, biodegradable and eco-friendly, with all the natural benefits of wool too.

Jo kindly sent me lots of photos and I was hooked, it didn't take much! We kept in contact after her commission piece was done and it was only a matter of time before we arranged to have two of her older ewes retire with me, Salt and Ava. It was no surprise to Jon that they were going to join us, a bit of a fait accompli really. We arranged to meet up roughly halfway between our two locations and as soon as I saw those tiny girls I was completely bowled over. There they were, bold as brass, standing in the back of Jo's truck, looking at me as though it was the most natural thing in the world to them. She had also been kind enough to bring me several Ouessant fleeces to work with, as well as some from other breeds like Blue Texel and Suffolk which really got me into working on ideas for my crafting.

Salt and Ava found their way into my heart very quickly and the Ouessant became one of my favourite breeds, along with the Herdwick. They might be tiny but they have the biggest personalities, are friendly and as I discovered, incredibly fast on their feet if you need to catch them.

One day, I noticed Salt was limping, guessing she probably had some mud stuck between her toes, I set off to catch her and sort it out. She had other ideas, her limp suddenly disappeared as I reached out to capture her, she went off like a rocket but unfortunately for me, I had just got hold of her and her speed took me straight off my feet, planting me face down in the wettest, muddiest part of the field with all the grace of a hippopotamus belly flopping into a pool. Salt meanwhile dashed off into the distance with no sign of a limp and I swear I could hear her laughing as she stopped at a safe distance to look back at me. Lesson learned, if you want to catch a reluctant Ouessant, use a rich tea biscuit to convince it wants to go into an enclosed area first!

The following year, I felt the need for more Ouessants so I got in touch with Jo to see if she would have any available after lambing season. By the end of that conversation, I realised I was possibly addicted as one ewe lamb had become a ewe lamb, an adult ewe and two wethers. The only problem was that, yet again, Jon had no idea of the impending arrival of more sheep. It was time for another one of those chats that went something like this, "Jon, seeing how much I've enjoyed working with the Ouessant fleece and it's gone well in the business, I was thinking it might be worth having another one to join the flock. They don't need much space and Jo does have a lamb coming up for sale." He gave me a sideways look, he'd probably already guessed it wouldn't be one and muttered "OK", admittedly looking unconvinced. A few days later, I told him I'd spoken to Jo and that she had a black ewe looking for a home, he looked at me sighed and gave in! That only left another two to tell him about and the night before we went to collect them, he asked how many we were picking up, he must have been suspicious already. I confessed that there were a couple of wethers coming too, but that only made four and size-wise that was barely a whole sheep compared to my Suffolk crosses. He wasn't overly convinced by my reasoning but neither was he shocked by the news and so Crystal, Mary-Kate, Patrick and Mr Tumnus joined the flock.

Jo and I started to make plans to go to the North Somerset Agricultural show the following May with some of her flock and Crystal so that I could experience showing sheep for the first time. Unfortunately, the covid pandemic put paid to that and the show was cancelled because the country was on lockdown.

The pandemic made little difference to our daily life on the farm, we still had to see to the animals and considered ourselves incredibly lucky that we were still able to go out to do that. We don't socialise much, we rarely have time or are just too exhausted so that part of the lockdown didn't affect us either. We couldn't imagine what other people were going through, being so restricted in what they could do and the loss of life was so shocking.

Once lockdown ended things slowly returned to normal around us and life on the farm continued much as usual, taking care of livestock, haymaking, crop planting and harvesting. We were still complaining about the weather on a daily basis because it's never right, too wet, too hot, too everything.

Towards the end of the year I had lost Sweep, who had not been himself for a little while, although we hadn't been able to get to the root of the problem. It was extra hard because we never found out what was wrong with him, maybe it was his age but still, it's easier to bear if you know why you've lost them. Things were made so much worse when a couple of months later, I found Sooty had died in his shelter. I think he had just given up after the loss of his twin, he hadn't been the same since then. I was left feeling heartbroken and gloomy. I had barely had time to recover from the sadness of losing my first own-bred sheep when another curved ball came in my direction.

My Ouessant wether, Mr Tumnus, started showing signs of having urinary calculi, bladder stones, which is something that castrated males can be prone to, and rams too sometimes, it was the same thing that had taken Herdy from me. After a visit from our vet Lucy and an attempt at treatment (rarely successful), things weren't improving so we decided that an operation to insert a catheter was the only course of action left. I prayed it would work but soon into the operation we discovered that the problem may not have been calculi as the catheter wouldn't go all the way in, meaning that the issue could be something more sinister. At that point there was only one course of action to take and I had to let him go. I was absolutely devastated and I still miss him now, he was the loveliest chap. It had always been a possibility that the operation would not be successful, Lucy and I had discussed it at length before we started, but I had held on to the hope that it might have been.

Approaching my sixtieth birthday late in 2021, I came across an advert for a little brown ram lamb, he looked very nice and my mind started to wander. Tentatively, I mentioned this little chap in conversation and to my amazement, (perhaps shock), Jon asked if I'd like him for my birthday. No surprises at my answer and a few calls later, we set off to Cornwall to meet Val Grainger and collect Jean-Paul. Val and I got on like a house on fire and her immense amount of knowledge about goats, sheep of many breeds and wool was more than impressive and we are still in regular contact, as I am with Jo.

It was safe to say that by now, I was truly addicted to Ouessant sheep, the following year adding another ten, six from Val, Rionach and her lamb, Morwenna, Molly (possibly the loudest sheep in the world, I swear Val can still hear her in Cornwall) with her lamb Marcell, Noggin the Nog and Jimmy Mintsauce and another four from Jo, Owlett, Skye, Astra and Clio. I even got involved with the breed enough to become a Trustee for the Breed Society for a while, an interesting experience, which is one way of putting it. Poor Jon is resigned to the fact that I could ask him to take me to collect more at any given time, but he is actually safe for now, I have plenty to be going on with!

The arrival of the last little group has been the real start of the future for me and my flock of Ouessants, along with their larger companions, with plenty of ideas and plans to move the craft business forward with more tutorials, workshops and new items made from the wonderful Ouessant fleece, all with no harm to the sheep.

Looking back, I would never have imagined that I would end up a shepherdess with a little fibre flock that I love dearly and a growing craft business, not to mention venturing into book writing! Life takes so many twists and turns, mine has taken me in a totally different direction to the one I expected it to. Yes, I do have some regrets, who doesn't, but starting with sheep is most definitely not one of them and is probably one of the best things I've ever done. Whenever it all seems too much or I'm feeling low, a bit of time with the flock, makes me feel so much better.

TO SOME THEY'RE JUST SHEEP,

TO ME, EVERYTHING.

Ava Heading Up The Ouessant Ewes

(Salt is on the left, closest to the hedge)

Ouessant Ewes

Astra, Skye, Clio and Owlett

Crystal

Jean-Paul

Rionach

Jimmy And Noggin

Owlett

Ouessants In The Frost

Molly and Marcell (front), Owlett and Morwenna

Patrick

Mary-Kate

Marcell In The Frost

Buddy The Herdwick

Spice

Buddy With The Triplets,

Siggy, Tristan and Treacle

Babs

Sugar

Printed in Great Britain
by Amazon

18667312R00068